T0387363

WHO'S HOO? OWLS!

Barred Owls

by Rachael Barnes

BLASTOFF! READERS
2

BELLWETHER MEDIA • MINNEAPOLIS, MN

Blastoff! Readers are carefully developed by literacy experts to build reading stamina and move students toward fluency by combining standards-based content with developmentally appropriate text.

Level 1 provides the most support through repetition of high-frequency words, light text, predictable sentence patterns, and strong visual support.

Level 2 offers early readers a bit more challenge through varied sentences, increased text load, and text-supportive special features.

Level 3 advances early-fluent readers toward fluency through increased text load, less reliance on photos, advancing concepts, longer sentences, and more complex special features.

★ **Blastoff! Universe**

Reading Level

    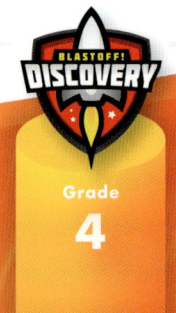

Grade **K**

Grades **1–3**

Grade **4**

This edition first published in 2025 by Bellwether Media, Inc.

No part of this publication may be reproduced in whole or in part without written permission of the publisher. For information regarding permission, write to Bellwether Media, Inc., Attention: Permissions Department, 6012 Blue Circle Drive, Minnetonka, MN 55343.

Library of Congress Cataloging-in-Publication Data

LC record for Barred Owls available at: https://lccn.loc.gov/2024000768

Editor: Christina Leaf   Series Designer: Brittany McIntosh   Book Designer: Veah Demmin

Printed in the United States of America, North Mankato, MN.

Table of Contents

Hidden in the Trees

Barred owls live in North American forests and **swamps**. They are named for their striped bellies.

They are known for
hoots that sound like,
"Who cooks for you?"

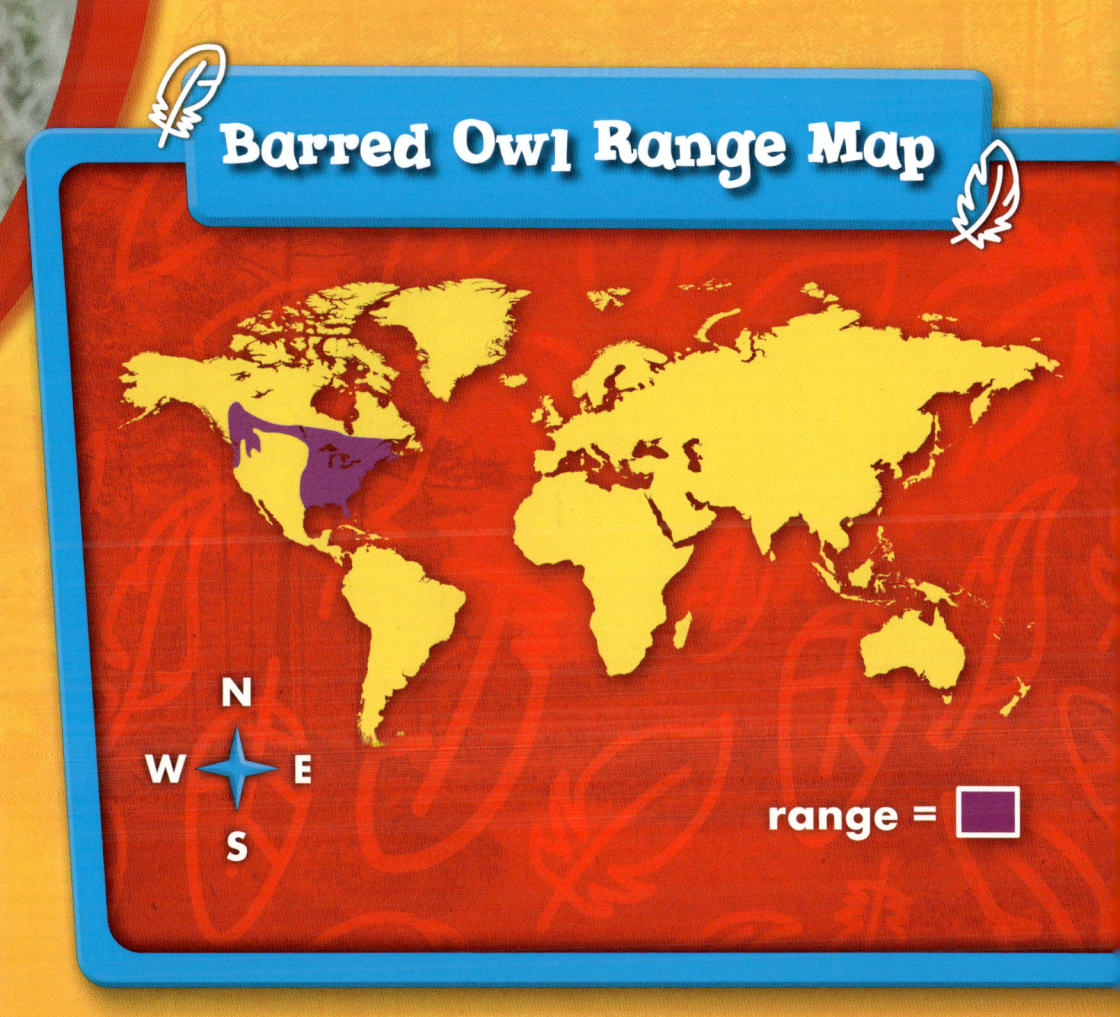

Barred Owl Range Map

N
W E
S

range =

Barred owls are large. Their **wingspan** reaches nearly 4 feet (1.2 meters) wide!

6

They can be
up to 20 inches
(51 centimeters) tall.

Barred Owl Wingspan

0   1 foot   2 feet   3 feet   4 feet

nearly 4 feet (1.2 meters) wide

Barred owls' feathers blend into their forest homes.

Brown and white feathers cover barred owls' bodies. Light brown feathers cover their faces.

9

yellow beak

Barred owls have
big, dark brown eyes.
Their beaks are yellow.

Their wings and tails are rounded. Their heads are round, too!

Spot a Barred Owl!

big, dark brown eyes

round head

brown and white feathers

Barred owls eat many small animals. **Rodents** and birds are common **prey**.

These owls will walk into **shallow** water to find food. They hunt fish and frogs.

prey

12

Barred Owl Food

rodents   birds   frogs

13

talons

These owls mostly hunt at night. They **dive** silently from **perches**. They grab prey with their sharp **talons**.

They can swallow
small food whole!

Barred owls watch
for danger. They hoot
and dive at animals
that get too close.

predator

Great horned owls are their main **predators**.

Born to Fly

Barred owls live in pairs
near water. They often use
holes in tall trees as nests.

Females usually lay two or three eggs each year.

nest

19

Owlets soon **hatch**. Older owlets are good climbers.

They jump between high branches to practice flying. At six weeks old, they learn to fly!

Growing Up

1 egg
about 1 month

2 owlet
about 6 weeks

3 fledgling
about 10 months

life span: up to 10 years

owlets

Glossary

dive—to fly down quickly

hatch—to break out of an egg

owlets—baby owls

perches—places to sit or rest above the ground

predators—animals that hunt other animals for food

prey—animals that are hunted by other animals for food

rodents—small animals that gnaw on their food; mice, rats, and squirrels are all rodents.

shallow—not deep

swamps—wet areas of land that are filled with trees and other woody plants

talons—the strong, sharp claws of owls and other raptors

wingspan—the distance from the tip of one wing to the tip of the other wing

To Learn More

AT THE LIBRARY

Neuenfeldt, Elizabeth. *Barn Owls*. Minneapolis, Minn.: Bellwether Media, 2024.

Whipple, Annette. *Whooo Knew? The Truth About Owls*. New York, N.Y.: Reycraft Books, 2020.

Wilson, Mark. *Owling: Enter the World of the Mysterious Birds of the Night*. North Adams, Mass.: Storey Publishing, 2019.

ON THE WEB

FACTSURFER

Factsurfer.com gives you a safe, fun way to find more information.

1. Go to www.factsurfer.com.

2. Enter "barred owls" into the search box and click 🔍.

3. Select your book cover to see a list of related content.

Index